SOUTH AFRICA
THE CULTURE

Domini Clark

A Bobbie Kalman Book

The Lands, Peoples, and Cultures Series

 Crabtree Publishing Company

The Lands, Peoples, and Cultures Series
Created by Bobbie Kalman

Revised edition: Plan B Book Packagers

Coordinating editor: Ellen Rodger

Copy editor: Adrianna Morganelli

Proofreader: Crystal Sikkens

Project editor: Robert Walker

Production coordinator: Katherine Kantor

Project development: First Folio Resource Group, Inc.
  Pauline Beggs
  Tom Dart
  Kathryn Lane
  Debbie Smith
  Tara Steele
  Robyn Craig

Design: David Vereschagin/Quadrat Communications

Consultants
Leon Jordan and Claudina Ramosepele, South African High Commission; Dr. Joseph R. Manyoni, Department of Sociology and Anthropology, Carleton University; Tshepoeng Mohohlo, Principal, Uitspandoorns Farm School; Professor T. Sono, Professor Extraordinary, Graduate School of Management, University of Pretoria and President, South African Institute of Race Relations; Michael Titlestad, University of South Africa

Photographs
AP/Wide World Photos: p. 10 (right); Corbis/Agence France Presse: p. 30 (bottom); Corbis/Charles O'Rear: p. 3; Corbis/Ted Spiegel: p. 13 (top); M. Courtney-Clarke/Photo Researchers: p. 17 (right); Gerald Cubitt: p. 8 (right); Wessel du Plooy/Shutterstock Inc.: title page; Jillian Edelstein/Link: p. 30 (top); Orde Eliason/Link: p. 5 (bottom), 16 (top); Elli/Shutterstock Inc.: p. 15 (bottom); David Garry/Shutterstock Inc.: cover, p. 22; Ingrid Gavshon/Link: p. 13 (bottom); Tom and Michele Grimm/International Stock Photo: p. 26 (top); Pierre Hollander/Link: p. 18 (right); Jason Lauré: p. 5 (right), 6 (left), 7 (top), 8 (top), 9 (bottom), 12 (both), 16 (bottom right), 19 (both), 21 (top), 22 (bottom), 23 (all), 24 (bottom), 25; Susan McCartney/Photo Researchers: p. 4 (top); Ruth Motau/Lauré Communications: p. 10 (left); Sean Nel/Shutterstock Inc.: p. 9 (top); Richard Olivier/Link: p. 11 (top); Billy Paddock/Impact: p. 11 (bottom); Caroline Penn/Impact: p. 27; Mark D. Phillips/Photo Researchers: p. 21 (bottom); PhotoSky 4t com/Shutterstock Inc.: p. 4 (bottom); Carl Purcell: p. 5 (bottom); Philip Schedler/Link: p. 15 (middle), 17 (left), 20; Tropix/A. Mountain: p. 14; Paul Weinberg/Impact: p. 26 (bottom); Ingrid Marn Wood: p. 6 (right), 7 (bottom), 15 (top), 24 (top); Andrew Verster: p. 31 (left)

Illustrations
Marie Lafrance: icon, p. 28–29
David Wysotski, Allure Illustrations: back cover

Cover: These colorfully painted huts on a beach in Cape Town are used as changing rooms by swimmers. The suburbs and area surrounding Cape Town have some of the most beautiful beaches in the country.

Title page: A troupe performs traditional dances at an event.

Icon: Hand woven baskets appear at the head of each section.

Back cover: The springbok is South Africa's national symbol.

Library and Archives Canada Cataloguing in Publication

Clark, Domini, 1979-
    South Africa : the culture / Domini Clark. -- Rev. ed.

(The lands, peoples, and cultures series)
Includes index.
ISBN 978-0-7787-9292-5 (bound).--ISBN 978-0-7787-9660-2 (pbk.)

    1. South Africa--Civilization--Juvenile literature. 2. South Africa--Social life and customs--Juvenile literature. I. Title. II. Series: Lands, peoples, and cultures series

DT1752.C57 2008   j968   C2008-902626-8

Library of Congress Cataloging-in-Publication Data
Clark, Domini, 1979-
    South Africa. The culture / Domini Clark. -- Rev. ed.
        p. cm. -- (The lands, peoples, and cultures series)
    "A Bobbie Kalman book".
    Includes index.
    ISBN-13: 978-0-7787-9660-2 (pbk. : alk. paper)
    ISBN-10: 0-7787-9660-4 (pbk. : alk. paper)
    ISBN-13: 978-0-7787-9292-5 (reinforced library binding : alk. paper)
    ISBN-10: 0-7787-9292-7 (reinforced library binding : alk. paper)
    1. South Africa--Civilization--20th century--Juvenile literature. I. Title. II. Series.

DT1752.C57 2008
968.05--dc21
                                        2008017484

Crabtree Publishing Company
www.crabtreebooks.com   1-800-387-7650

Published in Canada
Crabtree Publishing
616 Welland Ave.
St. Catharines, ON
L2M 5V6

Published in the United States
Crabtree Publishing
PMB16A
350 Fifth Ave., Suite 3308
New York, NY 10118

Published in the United Kingdom
Crabtree Publishing
White Cross Mills
High Town, Lancaster
LA1 4XS

Published in Australia
Crabtree Publishing
386 Mt. Alexander Rd.
Ascot Vale (Melbourne)
VIC 3032

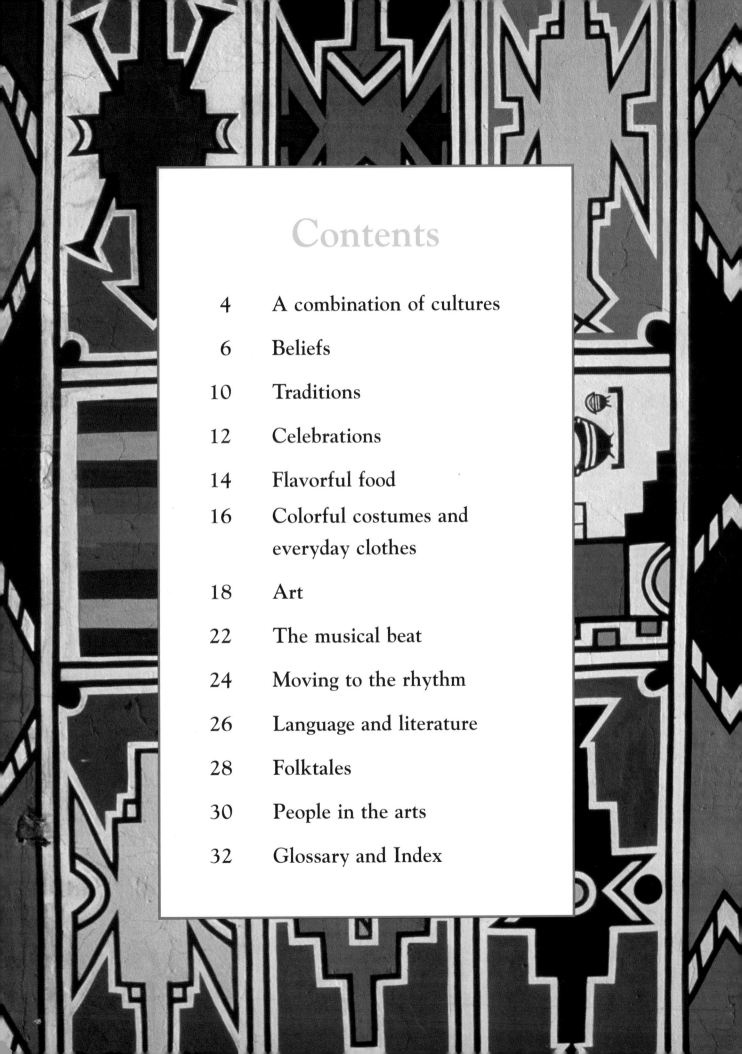

Contents

A combination of cultures

South Africa is a mix of peoples and cultures. Some people are **descendants** of the first humans who lived here 20,000 years ago. Others, such as the Zulu, Xhosa, Ndebele, and Venda, trace their roots back to the Bantu-speaking peoples who came to South Africa about 1,000 years ago.

(above) A Ndebele woman paints the walls of her home. Next, she will fill in the white areas with brilliant colors.

(right) South Africa is a modern country with both European and African traditions and customs.

From far away

South Africa is also home to people whose **ancestors** came from Europe, Southeast Asia, and India. The Afrikaners are a mixture of the Dutch, French, and German settlers who first came to the country in the 1600s. The Malay people were brought from Southeast Asia to work on the Afrikaners' farms. The British arrived in the 1800s, and brought Indians to work on their sugar **plantations**. Today, people still move to South Africa from other parts of the world.

Old and new

The many peoples of South Africa have added to the richness of the country's culture. Art, music, dance, food, and religion play an important part in each group's life, although their beliefs, traditions, and **customs** differ.

South Africa's culture is exciting and varied. Children watch cartoons on TV, but also listen to the tales of their **elders**. People are as likely to eat the foods of their ancestors as they are to indulge in fast food. Musicians play modern music, but they still use traditional African instruments. This mix of old and new makes South Africa a very interesting place!

(right) An actress dressed as an **isangoma**, *a traditional healer, sings a song in* **isiZulu**, *the language of the Zulu people.*

(left) Women in cone-shaped hats dip to the beat as they dance in a line.

Religions such as Christianity, Hinduism, Islam, and Judaism are all part of life in South Africa. So are beliefs that have been passed down from generation to generation, over thousands of years. Some people mix their beliefs. For example, many black South Africans who practice Christianity also consult the spirits of their ancestors about their everyday lives.

Traditional beliefs

According to the traditional beliefs of many black South Africans, one Supreme Being created everything in the world. Different South African cultures have different names for this Supreme Being. They all believe, however, that the creator of the universe does not control what happens day-to-day. People's ancestors are responsible for their families' daily lives. If the ancestors are happy, their families' lives will be happy. If the ancestors are angry, they will cause their families harm. They may make crops fail or bring illness to their families. People honor their ancestors with **rituals** and ceremonies to keep them content.

(above) At the market, customers can choose from many plants and herbs at this **inyanga's** *display.*

(left) An **inyanga** *and her student prepare medicine.*

6

Traditional medicine

When some people become ill, they consult traditional healers. A healer called an *isangoma* helps sick people by talking with their ancestors. The *isangoma* finds out why the ancestors are unhappy, then tells those who are ill the rituals to perform to make their ancestors happy again. Sick people might also visit an *inyanga*, or **herbalist**. An *inyanga* uses plants to cure aches and pains. Some healers, known as *umthakatis*, have a special skill that was passed on by older family members. Some know how to set bones, others know how to heal snakebites, and others help deliver babies.

Healers use the special ingredients sold in this herb shop for their treatments.

Traditional and modern

Today, healers and medical doctors work together and learn from each other to improve people's health. Before surgery, healers teach patients rituals in which they ask for energy from the Supreme Being. Doctors teach healers about serious illnesses and diseases so they can recognize their signs and give people better care. Drug companies consult with herbalists about the plants they use to cure illnesses and ailments. Some of these plants are now used in medicines around the world.

Bones, shells, bark, and other ingredients are used to heal aches and pains.

Christianity

There are many Christian churches around the world, such as the Catholic, Methodist, Baptist, and Anglican churches. All Christians believe that there is one God. They follow the teachings of Jesus Christ, whom they believe was God's son on Earth. Jesus' life and lessons are recorded in a holy book called the New Testament.

The oldest Christian group in South Africa is the Dutch Reform Church. This church dates back to the 1600s, when the Dutch first came to South Africa. One of the main beliefs of the Dutch Reform Church is that people's lives are planned even before they are born. The largest group of Christian churches in South Africa is the African Independent Churches, or the AICs. This organization of over 4,000 churches serves more than 10 million black people in urban and rural areas. The Zion Christian Church is the largest of the AICs. Its services include many rituals and ideas gathered from traditional beliefs.

(above) A Christian procession winds its way through a village to the chapel.

(right) Pictures of Hindu gods hang in the Indian market in Durban.

Hinduism

Most Indians in South Africa practice Hinduism. Hindus believe in many gods. Every day, they offer their gods gifts of flowers and fruit at small **altars** in their homes and temples. Hindus also believe that when people die, their souls come back in other forms. What form they come back in is determined by their **karma**, or how they behaved in their previous life. Hinduism is based on several books of ancient writings, including the four *Vedas*, the *Mahabharata*, the *Ramayana*, and the *Puranas*. These ancient writings are full of songs, poems, prayers, and legends.

Islam

Some Indians and Malays are Muslims. Their religion is Islam. Muslims follow the teachings of God, known as *Allah*. *Allah*'s instructions are written in the *Qur'an*, the Muslim holy book. There are five main principles, known as the Five Pillars of Islam. First, Muslims must declare that *Allah* is the only God and that Muhammad is his **prophet**. They must pray five times a day and give charity to the poor. During the holy month of Ramadan, Muslims must **fast** from dawn to dusk. Finally, those who can, must make a **pilgrimage** to the holy city of Mecca in Saudi Arabia, where Muhammad was born.

Judaism

Jews have lived in South Africa since the late 1800s. They fled Eastern Europe, where they were forbidden to practice their religion. Judaism is over 4,000 years old. The early history of the Jewish people and their main teachings are recorded in the *Torah*, the Jewish holy book. These teachings include the belief that there is only one God and that people should treat others as they would like to be treated.

(above) Dutch Reform churches are found throughout South Africa.

(below) Muslims say their afternoon prayers outside the oldest mosque in Cape Town.

Like people all over the world, South Africans honor important moments in family life, such as a child reaching adulthood, marriage, or death, with special events and celebrations. Some traditions have been passed down through many generations. Others are newer customs that reflect the changing lifestyles of many South Africans.

Baptism

Baptism is an important event for Christians. It is a way for them to show their belief in God, Jesus Christ. In some churches, people are baptized when they are infants. Other churches baptize teenagers and adults who want to show their commitment to their beliefs and to the church. Baptism is the act of either sprinkling holy water on a person's forehead while saying a blessing, or sometimes quickly dunking a person under water. In South Africa, some churches perform baptisms in rivers or in the sea.

After being circumcised, a Xhosa teenager sits quietly with a blanket over his head and clay smeared on his face.

Rites of passage

Each South African culture has a set of rituals that mark when a young person "comes of age," which means that the person is now considered an adult. The *domba*, or python dance, of the Venda people is a coming-of-age ritual for teenage girls. The girls dance in winding lines to the beat of drums. The Venda believe that the *domba*, which can last all night, helps ensure that rains will fall in the coming year.

When Xhosa boys reach puberty, usually around the age of thirteen, elders train them to be men. For three months, the boys learn about the history of their people and undergo survival tests. This period ends with a **circumcision**, followed by a feast and ceremony, to which the whole village is invited.

A member of the Zion Christian Church is baptized by being dunked in a river.

Members of the bridal party at a Malay wedding pose for the wedding photographer.

Getting married

Many South African weddings take place in a church, mosque, or synagogue, similar to weddings in North America. Some traditional weddings involve a **dowry**. The bride's parents offer a gift of useful household objects and clothes, which their daughter gives to her new husband. In some African cultures, the groom also gives a dowry, or *lobola*, to the bride's father in return for the bride's hand in marriage. The *lobola* is a way of making up for the loss that the girl's family feels, since she will go to live with her husband. The *lobola* used to be a gift of cattle, a sign of wealth among many African peoples, but is now often a gift of money.

Mourners lower a coffin covered with a blanket into the ground.

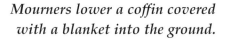

 # Celebrations

South Africans celebrate their beliefs and cultures throughout the year. Each **ethnic group** has its own holidays and festivals, but there are also many occasions that everyone celebrates.

(above) All South Africans celebrate Heritage Day. On this day, each ethnic group celebrates its history in its own way. At the Somerset West Festival, Afrikaners remember Jan Van Riebeeck, the first Dutch settler in South Africa.

(below) Crowds of children dress in costume for Cape Town's New Year's festival.

Easter

Easter is the most important Christian holiday. It marks the day on which Christians believe Jesus Christ rose from the dead. South African Christians celebrate Easter in a variety of ways. One celebration causes huge traffic jams around Moria in Northern Province. Every year, over one million followers of the Zion Christian Church make their way to Moria for Easter celebrations. For four days they do not eat. The pilgrims spend their time dancing, praying, and singing.

Diwali

The Hindu festival of Diwali honors Lakshmi, the goddess of wealth, beauty, and happiness. On this holiday, people place lit candles or oil lamps, called *dipas*, in windowsills, in doorways, along paths, and on the edges of buildings. They believe that if their home is lit, Lakshmi will offer them a special blessing. With all these lights, it is not surprising that Diwali is also known as the Festival of Lights!

The High Holidays

The High Holidays, Rosh Hashanah and Yom Kippur, are two of the most **sacred** Jewish holidays. Rosh Hashanah is the Jewish New Year. It is also the beginning of a ten-day period during which people ask others to forgive them for their sins. These ten days end with Yom Kippur, the Day of Atonement. It is said that on this day, God writes the names of all those who asked for forgiveness in the "Book of Life." These people will have a good and healthy year.

New Year's Day

January is in the middle of South Africa's summer. On January 1, New Year's Day, people fill the beaches and have barbecues, known as *braais*, with their families and friends. In Cape Town, people celebrate not only New Year's Day but also the day after, which they call *Tweedenuwejaar*, or Second New Year. People line the streets to watch parades of singers dressed in colorful costumes. The parades wind their way to a stadium where judges award prizes to the best musical acts.

(above) The **shofar,** *an instrument made out of a ram's horn, is blown during the High Holidays.*

(below) Men of the Zion Christian Church gather to hear a sermon during the Easter celebrations at Moria.

13

Flavorful food

Many different types of food from a variety of cultures make up the **cuisine** of South Africa. No matter what your tastes, you are bound to find something you enjoy, from steak and eggs to spicy **curries**, tasty barbecues, and fresh fish.

One-pot dishes

South Africans began eating one-pot dishes hundreds of years ago. At that time, they only had enough wood to make a small fire, so they combined all the ingredients in one iron pot. Today, one-pot dishes are still popular.

A traditional one-pot dish made of **maize**, or corn kernels, is called *mieliepap* in Afrikaans. Corn kernels are ground into a thick porridge, then served with a variety of sauces. Another one-pot dish is curry, which Indians introduced to South Africa. Curry is a mix of meat and vegetables that is cooked in a hot and spicy sauce.

Cape cuisine

Cape cuisine is a style of cooking that began in the coastal city of Cape Town. It evolved from the cooking styles of the many different people who settled there. Dutch people made thick stews and soups, Germans used sausages in their cooking, the French used preserved fruit, and the Malays flavored their food with hot spices. All these elements appear in Cape cuisine.

A main course might be *bobotie*, a popular Cape cuisine dish made of minced beef or lamb flavored with curry and dried fruit, topped with bread or egg custard. *Bredie* is a stew made of spiced meat and vegetables cooked slowly in a cast-iron pot. Desserts include dates stuffed with almonds and *malva*, a delicious pudding made with milk, sugar, cream, and apricot jam.

(above) Since South Africa is surrounded by water on three sides, there is plenty of fresh sea food. These women search for octopus trapped in rock pools and pry mussels off rocks during low tide.

14

(left) Roasted corn makes a tasty afternoon treat!

(below) Stewed fruit, pumpkin, eggplant, and other scrumptious South African dishes are traditionally cooked in heavy cast-iron pots.

Boerekos

The traditional food of the Afrikaners, whose ancestors came to South Africa as farmers, is called *boerekos*, or farmers' food. Farmers needed a lot of food to give them enough energy for a hard day's work. A typical breakfast includes several eggs, a steak, and a pile of bacon. At lunch or dinner, people eat vegetables cooked in sugar and butter, along with *boerewors*. *Boerewors* are sausages made with a variety of meats and spices. Vendors sell *boerewors* on streets, much like they sell hot dogs in North America. If people are not too full after dinner, they might finish their meal with a braid-shaped donut, called a *koeksister*, covered in syrup.

South African barbecues, called **braais**, *often feature meats such as boerewors, a type of sausage.*

Geelrys

Geelrys is a rice dyed yellow with a spice called turmeric. People have eaten this dish for many centuries. Here are the ingredients you will need to feed two to four people:

500 mL (2 cups) boiling water
250 mL (1 cup) rice
1 stick of cinnamon
2.5 mL ($\frac{1}{2}$ tsp) turmeric
5 mL (1 tsp) salt
5 mL (1 tsp) sugar
15 mL (1 tbsp) butter
125 mL ($\frac{1}{2}$ cup) raisins

Place all the ingredients except the raisins in the boiling water. Cook over low heat for twenty minutes. Add the raisins and turn off the stove. Leave the pot covered for ten minutes until the raisins get plump. Serve hot, and enjoy!

Colorful costumes and everyday clothes

South Africa is a modern country with people from many backgrounds. The clothing people wear every day reflects this variety. In the streets of Johannesburg, people are dressed in business suits. In small towns or villages, they wear T-shirts with shorts, jeans, or skirts. People also wear the traditional costume of their ethnic group. Some wear this clothing every day, while others wear it only on special occasions.

(right) Most young South Africans wear clothes like these – just like the clothes worn by young North Americans.

These Xhosa men wear brightly colored blankets even on warm days.

Traditional clothing

Each group of South Africans has a unique style of traditional clothing. The outfits are usually elaborate and colorful. Intricate hairstyles, colorful beads, and heavy jewelry adorn the women. Men might wear animal skins or colorful cloaks.

A Xhosa woman dressed in colorful clothing carries a traditional pipe.

Ndebele women may wear up to 35 kilograms (55 pounds) of jewelry! They never take off the stacks of copper rings around their necks and ankles.

What clothes tell

Often, clothing gives information about the people wearing it. It tells what ethnic group they belong to, whether they are Tembu, Zulu, or Venda. A costume also indicates how important a person is. For example, in Zulu society, only those with high status can wear animal skins. Healers, who are important in many societies, wear layers of skins and furs and special beaded necklaces.

Some clothing indicates whether a person is married or not. For example, in some groups, such as the Zulu and Xhosa, unmarried women wear short skirts while married women wear long ones.

 Art

From the rock art of early **nomadic**, or traveling, people to today's modern paintings and sculptures, South Africans have used art to show the beauty of their country, to tell about life around them, and to express their feelings. Traditional crafts such as hand-woven cloths, baskets, pottery, and jewelry are still made today for special ceremonies, for decoration, for everyday use, and for sale to tourists.

Rock art

The San and Khoikhoi people who lived in South Africa thousands of years ago hunted and gathered plants for food, then moved when there was no more to eat. They used the sandstone caves and shelters where they lived as a canvas for their rock paintings and carvings. Today, you can still see their detailed pictures in caves across the country, especially in the Drakensberg and Cape Mountains. Some of their pictures of animals, hunting trips, battles, and ritual dances are 20,000 years old.

Dangers to the rock art

Much of the rock art that remains is being damaged. Water and wind erode the rock's surfaces. Paint flakes off and carvings become less visible. Some people who visit caves with rock art damage the paintings without realizing it. When they touch the art, oils from their skin cause the images to fade. People splash water on the pictures to brighten them, but this only makes them lighter over time. Other people ruin the art on purpose by writing on it. Today, there are laws to protect rock art in national parks and reserves. Without this art, a great deal of information about the early peoples of South Africa will be lost.

(above) To make paint, the San mixed rock, sand, and plants with blood, milk, egg, white wine, or tree sap. Their paintbrushes were made from animal hairs, plant fibers, or feathers.

Wedding guests may buy these Venda dolls as a gift for the bride.

Dolls

South African dolls are very detailed and elaborate. The handmade wedding dolls of the Venda people are just one example. These dolls, which are given to brides as gifts, can be very small or they can be as tall as you are! The dolls are female figures with simple faces and long, cone-shaped bodies. They are decorated with many colors of fabric, silver rings, and beads, so each doll is unique.

Zulu beadwork

The Zulu are known for the beautiful beadwork they use in their clothing, to decorate dolls, and in jewelry. Sometimes, women string beads together to make an ankle bracelet. They send these bracelets to their boyfriends or husbands who are away from home, working in gold and diamond mines. Each color of bead has a different meaning. For example, red means love, yellow means home, and black means loneliness. By arranging the beads in different patterns, the Zulu send messages of love.

A Zulu woman wears a beaded headband and necklace.

Pottery

South Africans make pottery of all shapes and sizes. To make pots, they mold clay by hand, then smooth the clay with a piece of leather or a small hammer. Then, they leave the clay outside for several days to dry, or put it in an open fire so it can harden. For decoration, some people carve intricate details into the clay while it is still soft, or they paint the pot with geometric shapes after it cools. Pots are then used for carrying water, cooking, and storing food.

Weaving

South African groups such as the Venda, Sotho, and Zulu are known for weaving everything from baskets to fish traps and from clothing to blankets. They use various materials, including different types of grasses, straw, wool, cotton, and even telephone wire. Certain shapes in their weavings have special meanings. For example, in Zulu basketwork, a triangle means a man and a diamond means a woman. When two triangles or two diamonds are woven on top of one another, it means that a man or woman is married.

(opposite page) An artist carefully fills in color on a huge cloth painting.

(above) A common object is covered in Ndebele-style designs of paint and beads. Can you tell what it is?

(below) A woman weaves a basket out of reeds.

Music has always been important to South Africans. Music also played an important role in the struggle against **apartheid**, with some music even being banned because the government knew it had the power to unite and incite people to protest. Music in South Africa is a mix of traditional rhythms, melodies, and instruments, combined with modern sounds. South Africans play and listen to all kinds of music, including traditional music, jazz, gospel, opera, rock 'n roll, hip-hop, and dance music.

Jazz

South African jazz is famous worldwide. It began as a style of music called *marabi*. The musicians **improvised**, or made up, the music as they played together on any available instrument, from a piano to a can filled with stones. Over the years, guitars, bongos, drums, and **concertinas**, which are like accordions, became part of the sound. New musical influences came from the United States in the form of jazz, blues, and swing. These new sounds were added to the *marabi* style, along with local traditional rhythms, creating new forms of South African jazz.

Jazz musicians such as Hugh Masekela, Miriam Makeba, Abdullah Ibrahim, and Zim Ngqawana are known around the world for making music that reflects the cultural **diversity** of South Africa. Jazz became a symbol of protest and identity during the apartheid years and its popularity has continued to grow since the end of apartheid in 1994.

(top) A band plays traditional music at an outdoor event in Cape Town.

(bottom) Lively rhythms keep the musicians in this band moving.

Iscathamiya

South Africa is famous for *iscathamiya* music. A group of men, some with high voices and others with deep, low voices, sing together *a cappella*, which means there are no instruments. *Iscathamiya* developed from traditional Zulu singing and dancing contests. The lyrics are still sung in *isiZulu*, but added to the words are interesting sounds that have no meaning at all.

Johnny Clegg and Sipho Mchunu formed the popular group Juluka during apartheid, a time when people of different races were separated from one another.

A women's choir sings South Africa's national anthem Nkosi Sikelel' iAfrika.

Kwaito

Many young South Africans listen to *kwaito* music. Gritty lyrics about city life and violence are chanted or sung in local languages over programmed beats. *Kwaito* became very popular in the 1990s because it showed the youth across the country that they shared similar experiences, no matter where they lived or what language they spoke. South Africa also has its own hip-hop scene, where musicians speak to issues of poverty and inequality.

Instruments

South Africans play many different types of instruments. Some instruments are modern, such as synthesizers, bass guitars, and saxophones. Others are traditional. Bows are used for hunting or for playing music by plucking or striking the string. **Reed** flutes come in different lengths. Each flute has only one note, so you need a group to play a song. The *mbira*, or thumb piano, is made of short strips of metal or bamboo nailed to a wooden box. To play the *mbira*, you hold the box in both hands and pluck the strips with your thumbs, creating a soft, twangy sound.

 # Moving to the rhythm

South African dances often tell stories and describe past events. They are part of many celebrations and are also performed at tourist attractions. Most of the time, though, people dance just for fun!

Gumboot dance

In South Africa's gold and diamond mines, black miners were joined together with ankle chains so they could not escape. They were not allowed to speak while they worked, so they started the gumboot dance as a way of communicating with each other. The men made up a language by quickly stomping and slapping their high rubber boots, and jangling their ankle chains.

Now, children and adults perform the lively gumboot dance for fun, usually with no musical accompaniment. Dancers still wear boots and overalls like the miners, but they wear strings of bells instead of ankle chains.

Volkspele

The *volkspele*, which means "folk games," is a type of traditional Afrikaner folk dance. There are over a hundred different *volkspele* dances. Hundreds of couples can dance a *volkspele* at the same time, switching partners and performing spins called *tiekiedraais*.

(top) Afrikaners in traditional costume dance the **volkspele.**

(left) Performers dressed in miners' helmets and boots dance the gumboot dance at Gold Reef City, a reconstruction of what Johannesburg looked like during the gold rush.

Zulu dances

Young Zulu men perform a dance that celebrates their coming into manhood. The men dress in warrior costumes, with animal skins, fur headdresses, and beads. They also carry weapons during the dance. To the loud, strong beat of drums, the young men wave clubs and push shields made of cowhide out in front of them, as if they were fighting in a battle. This is done to show the chief that they are strong and skilled.

Zulu girls have dances of their own. Young Zulu girls wearing colorful bead headbands and costumes perform the reed dance for their families and friends. Each girl carries a tall reed as she parades in the dance, smiling to show that she is proud of who she is.

"I'll take your hand"

The Vulani Ringi Ring is a song and dance done by children. The chorus to the song is "You are my great big friend. I'll take your hand and dance in a ring with you." Children used to sing this song to their fathers when the men came home after being away for months working in the mines. Children have turned the dance into a game. A group of children holds hands in a circle and sings the song. When the children sing the words "great big friend," a child standing in the middle of the circle chooses a partner to spin around with. As the dance goes on, the children sing and spin faster and faster.

A dance troupe performs a loud and elaborate Zulu dance.

 # Language and literature

South Africa has eleven official languages: English, Afrikaans, *isiXhosa*, *isiZulu*, *isiNdebele*, *Sepedi*, *Sesotho*, *siSwati*, *Xitsonga*, *Setswana*, and *Tshivenda*. South Africans often speak three or more languages. Sometimes, they create new dialects. Kombuis Afrikaans, or "Kitchen Afrikaans," is a mixture of Afrikaans and English. Pidgin English is a mixture of English and a South African language.

(above) A sign in English and Afrikaans advises swimmers to watch out!

Click languages

Some languages, such as *isiZulu* and *isiXhosa*, have pop or click noises that people make with their tongues. There are different click sounds for different letters. Often, when these languages are written, an exclamation mark (!) is used to show where the click goes.

You make each click noise by moving your tongue in a certain way.

! For the letter "c," open your mouth slightly, put the tip of your tongue against the back of your top front teeth, and pull your tongue backward.

! For the letter "q," open your mouth, press your tongue hard against the roof of your mouth, then pull your tongue straight down.

! For the letter "x," open your mouth slightly, put your tongue against the back of your top front teeth, then pull your tongue across your molars on one side.

(left) Schoolmates try to read over their friend's shoulder.

English	Afrikaans	*isiXhosa*	*Tshivenda*	*isiZulu*
Hello	Hallo	Molo	Nda	Sakubona
Good morning	Goeiemore	Molo	Ndi matsheloni	Sakubona
How are you?	Hoe gaan dit?	Unjani?	No vuwa hani?	Unjani?
I am fine	Dit gaan goed	Ndiphilile	Ndi hone	Ngiyaphila
Good night	Goeienag	Rhonanai	Ndi madekwana	Salakahle
Good-bye	Tot siens	Hamba kakuhle	Salani zwavhudi	Hambakah
Yes	Ja	Ewe	Ee	Yebo
No	Nee	Xha	Hai	Cha
Please	Asseblief	Ndicela	Ndihumbela	Ngiyacela
Thank you	Dankie	Ndiyabonga	Ndolivhuwo	Ngiyabong

Afrikaans

Afrikaners and many other people whose ancestors worked on Dutch farms speak Afrikaans. Afrikaans comes from the Dutch language spoken by the early Dutch settlers. It also borrows from the languages of other people who lived in South Africa, such as the Africans, French, English, Malays, and Germans.

South African English

Many South Africans speak English, but their accents are probably not the same as yours and some of their vocabulary is different. For instance, an elevator is called a lift, and gas is called petrol. So many words are unique to South African English that the language has its own dictionary.

Writing

Authors writing in all of South Africa's languages have contributed to South Africa's culture. Their novels, magazine articles, and poetry have informed the people of South Africa about the events in their country. South Africans who write in English, or who have their work translated into English, have also been able to let people all over the world know what life is like in their country.

These girls catch up on the latest adventures of their favorite comic book hero.

Most of South Africa's stories are not written down. The people have an oral tradition, which means that tales are remembered and told by storytellers in each generation. The Zulu people have a whole group of tales about a **trickster** named Hlakanyana who always gets into trouble. Here is one of Hlakanyana's adventures.

Hlakanyana, the Zulu trickster

One sunny morning, Hlakanyana came across three birds caught in a trap. "My," he thought, licking his lips, "these birds would make a very tasty lunch." Hlakanyana pulled the birds from the trap and turned to head for home, but he could not move. Hlakanyana was stuck in the trap!

Suddenly, three hunters appeared. "Look!" they cried. "It's our lucky day. Three birds and a trickster in one trap – and just in time for lunch."

"Wait!" screamed Hlakanyana as the hunters pulled out their spears. "Just look at me! I'm very dirty. I'm going to taste terrible!"

The hunters laughed. "We can wait. We will clean you up, then we will eat well tonight."

The hunters took Hlakanyana home to their mother and then left to continue hunting. The mother scrubbed Hlakanyana from head to toe. Then, she made sure that he was tied up tightly, put on a pot of water to boil, and busied herself chopping vegetables. Hlakanyana looked fearfully at the pot, "I'll be cooking in there soon," he thought. Suddenly, he had an idea.

"You work so hard," he said to the mother. "Wouldn't you like to take a break and play a game?"

The mother did want to play a game, but she was suspicious. "What kind of game?" she asked.

"A fun one," said Hlakanyana with a grin. "We will take turns jumping in and out of that huge pot. Whoever can do it for longer wins." The mother thought that sounded like fun. She agreed to play the game and untied Hlakanyana.

"I'll go first to show you how it is done," explained Hlakanyana. He leaped into the pot with a splash, and then jumped out. He did it again, and again, and again. "Woah," he huffed, "I'm tired. That's all the jumping I can do. Now, it's your turn." The mother jumped into the pot, and then out. Over and over, she jumped, laughing the whole time. "You're good at this," observed Hlakanyana. "One more jump and you will win."

The mother jumped one more time into the pot of steaming water. This time, Hlakanyana slammed on the lid and sat on top of the pot until the mother was nicely cooked. Just as he was adding the vegetables to the mother soup, he heard the hunters returning home. Quickly, he ran to the closet and found some of the mother's clothes.

The hunters stormed into the house. "We're hungry!" they roared. Hlakanyana, disguised as the mother, served them the soup. The hunters slurped hungrily at the soup. They looked at each other. "This does not taste like trickster soup!" they bellowed. They grabbed Hlakanyana. He managed to wriggle free and sped out of the house.

The hunters ran after him. Hlakanyana was far ahead of them. Suddenly, he came to a wide river. He was trapped. What could he do? Hlakanyana had an idea. Using his special powers, he turned himself into a stick.

When the hunters arrived at the river, they looked everywhere for Hlakanyana. He was nowhere to be seen. Furious, one of the hunters picked up a stick and threw it into the river.

The stick, which was really Hlakanyana, floated down the river, away from the hunters. "That was a close call," thought the trickster as he changed back into himself. Hlakanyana noticed that the sun was starting to set. "There's just enough daylight to find something else to do," he thought. And off he went, in search of more trouble.

Great singers, artists, authors, and actors are heroes to South African people. This was especially true during apartheid, when artists used their talents and creativity to protest the unjust rules of the time. Apartheid was a system of laws in South Africa that separated people according to their skin color. White people had the most rights and black people had the fewest. Blacks and other non-white people were treated terribly under apartheid. The music, pictures, and words of South Africa's artists helped bring world attention to what was going on in their country under apartheid.

Miriam Makeba

Miriam Makeba was the first South African to make the music of her country internationally known. She started her career as a singer with bands that toured across South Africa. She later played the lead in a South African musical about a black boxer, called *King Kong*. After that, she starred in a film about apartheid called *Come Back Africa*, which brought international attention to the South African government. She was **exiled** from South Africa because of her role in the film. She returned to South Africa in the 1990, where she continued to record albums. In 2002, she appeared in the film *Amandla*, which documented the anti-apartheid struggle and how music was used as a form of protest.

Nadine Gordimer

Novelist and short-story writer Nadine Gordimer grew up in a small mining town near Johannesburg. When she was nine years old, she started writing about what it was like to be a white girl who disagreed with apartheid laws. At the age of fifteen, her writing was published for the first time in a Johannesburg magazine. Since then, her stories of people who lived through apartheid have been published around the world, although many were once banned in her own country.

Music lovers describe Miriam Makeba's voice as being "as deep as the Indian Ocean and as sparkling as the diamonds of her country."

Nadine Gordimer won the Nobel Prize for literature in 1991. Her writing was often banned during the apartheid era.

Zakes Mokae

One of South Africa's most famous actors is Zakes Mokae. He has starred in many Hollywood movies, such as *A Dry White Season* and *Cry Freedom*, and in plays such as South African playwright Athol Fugard's *Master Harold… and the Boys*. His career was strongly affected by apartheid. In 1961, Mokae toured South Africa with Fugard, performing together in *The Blood Knot*, a play about a white man and a black man who were brothers. Because of apartheid, the two actors had to travel in separate train compartments and sleep in different hotels.

Athol Fugard

Athol Fugard is a playwright and novelist with Afrikaner roots. Much of his work deals with the injustices of apartheid. He worked with black actors throughout his career and endured government restrictions and harassment because his plays were considered controversial. At one point, while working in England, the South African government withdrew his passport. Fugard is known for making his audiences think. His book Tsotsi was made into a film and won an Academy Award in 2005.

National Arts Festival

Throughout the year, South Africa has many music, art, and drama festivals. The largest is the National Arts Festival, held in the small city of Grahamstown in Eastern Cape. For ten days in July, thousands of people come to watch performances. Dancing, music, drama, poetry readings, and art are crammed into every nook and cranny of the town's restaurants, halls, schools, and streets. At the National Arts Festival, new artists have a chance to show their work to the people of South Africa. Young people are also encouraged to participate, and the best young artists receive awards.

Vusi Mahlasela

Writer Nadine Gordimer has described Vusi Mahlasela as a "national treasure". Mahlasela is a poet, songwriter, singer, and activist who writes about the reality of life in his country. Many of his songs deal with the sad years of apartheid, when friends and families were torn apart and many people were exiles in foreign countries. More recently, his subjects have included the many deaths in South Africa from HIV/AIDS. Mahlasela records and plays concerts throughout the world. He set up a music development foundation that preserves African musical traditions and brings music eduction to children in South Africa.

Andrew Verster

Andrew Verster is recognized around the world for the large number and variety of artwork he has created. Verster's prints and oil paintings, banners, and posters show how the people of South Africa felt while living under apartheid.

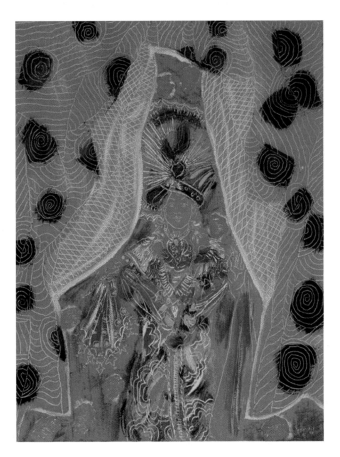

This oil painting by Andrew Verster is called **Sacred Images.**

Glossary

altar A table or stand used for religious ceremonies

ancestor A person from whom one is descended

apartheid A policy of separating people based on their race

baptism A ceremony that welcomes a person to the Christian church. During the ceremony, the person is dipped or washed in water, as a sign of washing away sin

circumcision Removing the foreskin of a penis

concertina A small musical instrument that looks like an accordion

cuisine A way of cooking or preparing food

curry A spicy dish of meat, fish, or vegetables

custom Something that a group of people have done for so long that it becomes an important part of their culture

descendant A person who can trace his or her family roots to a certain family or group

diversity Different kinds of people and cultures

dowry The money or property that a bride brings to her groom when they marry

elder An older person who is highly respected by his or her community

ethnic group People who share a common language, religion, and history

exile To force a person to leave his or her country or home

fast To stop eating food or certain kinds of food for religious or health reasons

herbalist A person who uses herbs to treat disease

improvise To make up as you go along, for example, a song or a speech

karma A person's thoughts and actions in a previous life that determine what the next life will be like

maize Corn

nomadic Having no fixed home and moving from place to place

pilgrimage A religious journey to a special place

plantation A large farm on which crops such as cotton and sugar grow

prophet A person who is believed to speak on behalf of God

reed The hollow stalk of a tall grass

ritual A religious ceremony in which steps must be followed in a certain order

sacred Having special religious significance

trickster Someone who plays tricks on others

 # Index

Printed in the U.S.A.